Marriage
A
Recipe
For
Divorce?

**The Hidden Ingredients of Western
Marriage are not on the Label
Could this be the cause of the 45%
divorce rate in our Culture?**

By: Heru EL

Marriage
A
Recipe
For
Divorce?

Copyright ©2018 by Heru EL
UAXSAKTUNPUBLISHERS Private Ltd.

uaxsaktunpublishers@gmail.com

Cover Artist: Visualgfx
Editor: Heru EL
First printing: July 2019
ISBN: 978-0-9843080-2-6
Ministry
Of
The Sacred Temple of the Veiled Traveler U.A.

Table of Contents

Preface..4

The Habits of Culture....................6

The Fertile Soil of Culture...........11

Loves Biological Ingredients.......20

Survival of our Species...............25

The Culture of Selection.............29

Rinse and Repeat.......................38

Changes on the Horizon?..........44

Conclusion..................................50

Bibliography...............................54

Preface

At the age of 3 years old, I came to the Midwestern city of Chicago, Illinois and as I grew up my mental visions and perceptions were shaped by the environments my parents placed my siblings and I in. I was fortunate to have both a mother and father present in my life who's mission was to give their children a better life then they had in contrast to the harsh life in Mississippi where the choice of jobs and career opportunities were scarce. I got my first exposure to family life and marriage from my parents, uncles' aunts and family friends. For the most part through the years that past most of them stayed married with the exception of just a few that I can remember I would say about 80% of them. I grew up and eventually graduated from high school, started a full time job and fell into what I thought was love. I remember at the age of 19 discussing my decision to get married with my father and he said "Oh boy! why do you want to do that so soon, why don't you travel the world and enjoy yourself" and he proceeded to tell me stories of his days in the Navy when he would travel from port to port and how his travels took him to countries like Belgium, France, Germany and Korea. It sounded intriguing but I was too far gone to even hear his words I couldn't wait to be in her arms every night in heavenly bliss. I along with most of my high school friends were all married within 3 years after High School. Within 10 years with the exception of one we were all divorced and that one couple is still married to this day. I was always the kind of person who hated defeat but also was interested in the how and why part of life's questions. This book breaks into the hidden parts of why my friends and I made those decisions and what was the driving catalyst that blindly compelled us to not only marry so young but some of us several times again. Some of you who will read this book may be able to recognize society's subliminal programs of how culture and traditions can cast you on board a runaway train without brakes which sounds rather scary. But what if you don't think you're on a runaway train.

The Habits of Culture

It's Saturday afternoon and the sounds of slow and melodic musical arrangements echo throughout the walls and stained glass windows of the church. The audience of well-dressed men, women and children on both sides of the aisle turn their heads towards the rear as the main participant of the ceremony is about to take her triumphant walk arm in arm with her father as he has conceded his will over his daughter and delivers the bride to her soon be husband where they will make public statements about how much they will commit to one another in their coming years. Tears stream down some of the faces of the witnesses as well as the bride as she makes her way to the altar. Her groom stands nervously waiting on her delivery by her father as her veiled face proceeds before him. Various colors of flowered petals dropped by the pretty little flower girl lay scattered on the floor as they slowly march by. The preacher/priest prepares to bestow his verbal blessings in the name of the State and God. Yes the drama and pageantry of western culture will replay this same scene throughout Europe, South America and all of North America. In the United States alone over 2 million couples each year will participate in this integral part of our culture. The bride and groom each equally confident that this is a match sealed with the blessing of God and in no way will entertain the thought of anything else but heavenly bliss as they whisk away to their honeymoon. Sounds like a lovely end to a ROMANTIC novel doesn't it? The bonds of culture, emotions and societal pressure often times are misleading when wise and prudent considerations should have been in order. But ROMANTIC love will be the number one guiding force that will thrust these participants into a world of the unknown. They were told time and time that love will conquer all no matter what. We will redress that later. This culturally phenomenal industry is called by some as the marriage industry, Industry? One may ask, one of the definitions of Industry is the following "a particular form or branch of economic or commercial activity". But why would I dare place such a sacred part of our culture in such a mundane category. Well I can only refer you to the trail of money in its wake. A whopping $72 billion dollars is generated each year from wedding ceremonies both large and small. Just to mention a few items, over $19 billion will be generated on gifts alone, $8 billion on honeymoons, over $6 billion on wedding rings, let's not forget the revenue from tuxedo's, wedding gowns, the rental of reception facilities, flowers alone generate $6 billion for this highly lucrative industry.

Invited guests and relatives need lodging, travel expenses to and from the wedding. Last rites ceremonies called bachelor, bridal parties as well as bridal showers prior to the wedding. You get the picture everybody gets a piece of this pie even the shoeshine boy, and we can't forget the liquor industry, there is no celebration in the America's without the spirits! Wow I'm sure somebody was left out but they know who they are. All in all it adds up to over $72 billion dollars in revenue and rising. When those 5 magical words slide through ones lips "Will you marry me" and that 1 word "yes" is answered, a ripple the size of a powerful tsunami is generated to the glee of "The Marriage Industry". This is not a seasonal ceremony this is nonstop from January to December with May to October getting the bulk of ceremonies. Yes that great generator called ROMANTIC love is something most of us will deal with in one way or another either supporters or participants. Just how good is this powerful energy we call Romantic Love at having a successful marriage? What is the track record? After all before you start such a life changing endeavor, one that will affect your family, friends and just about every phase of your life, what are the true dynamics of this undertaking that our culture has placed on the back of ROMANTIC love. Well so far we know love is an emotion so it in itself does not consider reason or common sense, it avoids things like probability for success. This love emotion basically just wants us to try to maintain this blissful state and ignore anything else. Let's consider some of the things ROMANTIC love does not want you to know about. In the United States alone the average marriage will end in divorce 45% of the time or 4.5 of the 10 marriages will end in divorce within 10 years. What about those who think they made a mistake the first time and tried it for the second time well it doesn't get any better the number goes up to 60%. So if you are planning on going to the altar for the second time your chances of failure is now 6 out of ten. If this is your 3rd time around, you're starting to get into winning the lottery odds, your failure rate just jumped to 73% "Ouch!" In the words of Samuel Johnson a famous playwright and poet "Remarriage is a Triumph of Hope over Experience" The average first marriage lasts 8 years, here is the sad part, 50% of all children will see their parent's divorce in their lifetime. Wow Romantic love is taking some serious hits. Well let's just walk out of the love section and into the common sense section of our minds and see what's on sale. If I were to suggest that we go to a restaurant and the probability that we would be served is 55% would you want to take a chance that the waiters would constantly walk by you and not even acknowledge you while you sit waiting and hoping that you didn't fall into 45% of patrons who would NOT be served. If you went shopping for a new car and the salesperson showed you two cars and one of the cars you absolutely "Loved" (there goes that emotion again) and another car which was not your dream car. The sales agent tells you the car you absolutely love has a 45% chance of breaking down within the year and the other car had a 4% chance of breaking down. Which factor would you use to make your choice, love or common sense? Well I'm sure some will rationalize that cars and food can't compare to true romantic love. I say to that "numbers don't lie". I say people take more care in selecting their houses and cars than spouses. So what is this driving force that we call ROMANTIC love that has wrapped its powerful tentacles around the DNA of the Western Occidental world of American Culture? Is it a concept, a trend or social engineering?

The Fertile Soil of Culture

You may be getting the feeling that I must somehow be against Love, quite the contrary, I am greatly appreciative that the Creator/Designer saw fit to give mankind this wonderful compassionate gift. Love is responsible for an unlimited amount of joy and wonderment in our lives. What I am focusing on is the misuse, miseducation, abuse and utter exploitation of this energy we are calling love. By this mass commercialization of Romantic love this Western Culture from Europe to the Americas has diluted the raw energy and power of love into the latest cover of Brides Magazine or the latest romantic novel or 2 minute love scene in a movie. The questions about love can multiply into infinity, here are a few. What is love? Why do people say love hurts? How do you fall into love? Can you fall out of love with someone you say you fell in love with? Can you kill over love? Can you love two people at the same time? There are millions in jail, hospitals and the cemetery who are victims of this confusing yet powerful energy as well as people in absolute bliss. There are people who are in love with people who they are absolutely in fear of, as well as people who they absolutely don't want to be in the same room with. This energy called love seems to have a mind of its own. But did we humans give it some of its devious yet sweet disposition. Most of the people who have been born in the past 120 years are born into the culture of ROMANTIC love especially in the western culture. Before we continue lets define these two words; **Culture** and **Western Culture**. From the Oxford Dictionary of English; "**Culture**, noun / *the ideas, customs, and social behavior of a particular people or society"* So the two words that seem to stand out to me is "ideas" and "social behavior" before you can have social behavior, the idea must be introduced and then slowly accepted which turns into a pattern and when enough people mimic this behavior it slowly turns into a customary activity which spreads from one network of people to another. We will come back to this soon. The next term you will find me referring to frequently is "**Western Culture**" as defined from Wikipedia; "*Is a term used very broadly to the heritage of social norms, ethnic values, traditional customs, belief systems (Christianity) and political systems that have some origin or association with Europe. The term also applies beyond Europe to countries that have been strongly connected to Europe by colonization, immigration or influence. The cornerstone of Western thought emanates from Greek and Roman ancient civilizations"* Well now that's over 2,000 years of customs and ideas. So when one is born into such a steep history of traditions and behaviors you are groomed from childhood to see these so called normal customs being repeated over and over again we don't question there validity especially at the tender and naive age of 4 years old, that's the average age of the ring bearer in an American wedding. Let's take a look at one aspect of this culture that you have noticed I have capitalized earlier and that is ROMANTIC love. In our impressionable years from infancy to adolescence we are bombarded with books, magazines, commercials, movies, television shows, the behavior of the nucleus of our families, friends as well as our observations of people. Our parents and grandparents have all been born in the last 100 years so this behavior has been spoon fed to us from infancy decade after decade. Don't blame them they were influenced by a new concept called Romantic love. I'm sure you've heard of an era in European history called the Renaissance, a period of time from late 1400s to the mid 1600's. French historian Jules Michelet defined the 16th century Renaissance as a period in Europe's cultural history that represented a break from the Middle Ages. This era introduced a distinct change in several categories in social behavior and resulted in the populous to be exposed to new and open expressions of art, science and philosophy that were not controlled by the church. In came the rise of the middle classes who were exposed to the same culture as the Nobles and Monarchies. Thanks to the printing press introduced in the late 1400s, previously unknown ideas were revealed to the middle classes who began to read and discern these new concepts and ideas. During this time period between the Renaissance late 1400s to the mid-1800s there were several influential philosopher's, authors playwrights and poets that where highly influential in attitudes about relationships between men and women. Sir Walter Raleigh, William Shakespeare to name a few. Stage plays would introduce the story of a hero who embarked on an adventure and sometimes these adventures included a chance meeting with a maiden from a distant and exotic land and they would have a passionate relationship and he would whisk her off on his white horse and off gallantly to his grand estate and they would live happily ever after in unlimited bliss. Well they called these *chivalric romance* plays which later turned into novels and novelettes. Up until the 1800s marriage was mostly an arranged affair especially by the monarch's and noble classes and the union of the bride and groom were for the advancement of the two families involved for the enrichment and advancement of each family line. If a wealthy ship builder had a daughter she would be matched with the son of a wealthy land baron. As a result of this alliance they have more power and political influence and now their children can be educated at the finest universities and the string of wealth, power and influence accumulated in those two respective houses as the children were so to speak be "married off". However the notion of love was something that was more likely between the husband and his mistress rather than his wife and the wives in those elite social circles also enjoyed their own fancies of lovers as well. The wife was expected to perform her so called wifely duties such sex on demand, grooming the children for success and maintain the reputation and status of the family name. With the advent of a growing middle class that dreamed of living like the wealthy and the poorer classes longing to live like the middle classes, social norms began to change quickly. But this notion that one can decide for his or her self who they should marry came through advent of plays and literature during the so called "Age of Enlightenment". More and more people were exposed to this new philosophy as the populations in Europe and a young United States were growing in the later 1800s just before the Industrial Age. I don't want to go into too much detail as to how the social development of these new ideas slowly changed the western cultures views on marriage it may bore you, for now let's examine the word called ROMANCE once more and see how it got entangled with love. Earlier I mentioned how romance novels had a pretty standard formula, strong, handsome, upper class noble or royal family prince goes off on a quest or adventure and in his travels he rescues or meets a beautiful maiden and they get married or she becomes his mistress and they live happily ever after. Let's go back to the definition of the word ROMANCE and you may be surprised to find its original meaning is rather different than today's meaning, from the American Dictionary of the English Language by Noah Webster 1828.

ROMANCE/ noun, romans', ro'mans. **1**. *A fabulous relation or story of adventures and incidents designed for the entertainment of readers; a tale of extraordinary adventures, fictitious and often extravagant, usually a tale of love or war. It <u>vaults</u> and <u>soars beyond</u> the limits of fact and real life.*

2. *A fiction; to forge and tell <u>fictitious stories</u>; to deal in extravagant stories.*

Ladies and Gentlemen, Girls and Boys, this in my opinion is the root cause of failure in what is properly defined as "Love Marriages" I know this slaps you in the face because you don't have any reference point to attach such a wild notion to. However if you will allow me to take your mind to a different point of view maybe I can bring some clarity to this subject. If we are honest about this in your personal experiences as well as our observance of friends and relatives, we all have this one story line that we think the man or woman of our dreams is supposed to fit into, notice I said story line. The first trap in seeking a wife or husband is that it must fit the "fantasy storyline" the man needs to be handsome and strong and a protector like a hero or gallant prince, and the woman has to be beautiful with certain attributes like long flowing hair, big beautiful eyes, and a shapely slim body and of course a pleasing personality. Then once that first step in the story is met, the adventure starts because after the first date leads to several more coupled with long hours on the phone or back in grandma's day a now forgotten art of love letters were written back and forth. Today it would be a series of text messages. Listening to each other's life stories (as least the stories they want you to know) and then finally it happens, you have sex and you both swear it is one of the best experiences of your life. You both end up saying things like, "This is too good to be true" or my favorite "No one has ever made me feel like this before". You go to places you've never been before, you plan trips together or should I say adventures. You both are having so much fun. When you have problems he or she comes to your rescue in times of need or comfort. You both long for each other, to touch, to hear, to smell and taste. You each tell your friends and relatives about your great interest and finally you meet each other's families and friends. You may hear a friend or family member who knows the real history jokingly say, "Do you know what you are getting yourself into" but you shrug it off as an inside family joke. She ignores her mother's advice of "I don't think he's the right one for you" "But mom I'm in love I can't live without him" and this is only after 6 months. So now what is the logical or should I say illogical next chapter in this story, most couples according to Brides.com online magazine August 2017 edition date for about a year then they move in together and 2 years later the wedding plans start on average 3 to 4 years after they met, many a lot sooner. Now they have to finish the story of happily ever after. Lord knows they are both tired of hearing family members pressure them with "don't you think it's time for him to pop the question?" "What is he waiting for?" Here is my question. Do they really want to get married or are they being compelled by custom or storyline. There are facades that are starting to crumble inside them as they try so hard not to scream out in a maddening outburst at each other's habits and they both promise to work on their bad habits, because they are told love will conquer all. Their friends and family are always asking how the relationship is going, they both tell half-truths and half lies because they have already told everyone these wonderful and fantastic stories of why this is the love of my life so they must make this fantasy story work. Remember one of the definitions of ROMANCE; *fictitious and often extravagant*. I read one story of how a man rented a white Rolls Royce and hired musicians and models and as his girlfriend stepped out of her office building she was met with the sound of trumpets blaring and a red carpet was rolled out and he gallantly positioned himself on one knee and proposed. How ROMANTIC was that! Less than 3 years later they were divorced. What I want you to ask yourself is, am I playing a character in a story that I feel compelled to play? When Valentine's Day rolls around couples are expected to play their parts and say something or do something ROMANTIC, because if you don't a different kind of hell will break loose, I have seen relationships fall apart because of it. What's driving these ROMANTIC adventures and as a famous line in a song once said "What you won't do, you'll do for Love" could it be something even more powerful than culture. Could it be biological? Let's find out.

Loves Biological Ingredients

You mean there's a science to this love energy? Oh yes indeed, many hours and research grants have been devoted to this topic. Some scientists have narrowed it down to 3 basic stages to falling in love. A recent study completed at Rutgers University of Brunswick, New Jersey based on the topic "Science behind the Love" revealed that the three stages are as follows, Lust, Attraction and Attachment. As a couple enters each stage unbeknownst to them there are different chemical reactions as well as different sets of hormones that are released in the brain and throughout the body with the most powerful hormones being released in the "attachment" stage. That's amazing since most of the Western world is highly fascinated with the notion that falling in love is some mystical magical cupid with wings that somehow strikes us with it arrow and we fall victim to its dictates. Our culture is full of romantic stories in all facets of media that drive home this fanciful story of happily ever after in love, but the story isn't finished when the screen or book says "The End". Let's examine these steps briefly. Number 1 **Lust**, plainly put, it is the sex drive or commonly called libido, the natural desire to have a physical or sexual union with the desired and appropriate partner. When one views a

person and immediately notices a desire
rising within them it is a result of two
hormones released in the brain, testosterone
and oestrogen most people think only men
have testosterone and women have
oestrogen (also spelled estrogen) however we
all have both in our bodies. So before we get
physical we get **chemical**. So these chemicals
trigger the domino effect which causes us to
place ourselves in a position to be noticed
and once we meet the object of your desire
and there is a mutual desire then that's when
the next phase begins. You begin to converse
and laugh and touch, smell, make eye contact
and this leads into step number 2, **Attraction,**
During this time which is usually called dating
not only is testosterone and oestrogen
involved but now the hypothalamus part of
the brain notices this may be getting serious
and it releases the hormone Dopamine which
gives us this feeling of pleasure when we
perform a certain task, like eating your
favorite food or favorite chocolate, you know
it's that hidden little voice in the back of our
minds that says "I like that lets do it again" so
when the kissing, cuddling and the sex starts
to happen in the relationship Dopamine and
its powerful cousins called Norepinephrine
and Vasopressin join together and release
high levels of these hormones into our bodies
which causes us to be more energetic and
euphoric, you know that energetic flush in
your face when your friends ask you "What
did you do last night?" This makes us want

more and more of this wonderful feeling we are getting from this person. You know this is the period where you're having sex like rabbits any time any place. Now isn't this starting to sound more and more like an addiction? Maybe, let's move on, so in time the relationship moves into step number 3, **Attachment,** So now we have 5 chemicals or hormones racing to and fro in our body, Testosterone, Oestrogen, Dopamine, Norepinephrine and Vasopressin. Now the party is getting serious now because the life of the party just showed up and its name is Oxytocin, believe me it is made for this moment. Very powerful because it introduces a feeling of "Bonding" much like the bond between a mother and her baby, but of course different in intensity. This is a powerful hormone secreted from the brain. In the woman her Oxytocin levels can skyrocket to 51% during orgasm. In men its counterpart Vasopressin takes a big leap in levels as well. In the science community Oxytocin is called the love hormone or cuddle hormone. During the dating period most couples engage in tons of sex and these five powerful hormones are constantly being secreted over and over again. Now they find themselves making the following statements; "I just couldn't take my mind off of you" and "I just can't stand being away from you" "Let's move in together" or "Let's get married" The bonding process is now complete and the final step of **Attachment** is at its apex. But let's take a closer look because men and women react differently from these hormones racing through their bodies. Earlier I noted that the Oxytocin levels during orgasm can rise as much as 51% in women after orgasm which research shows that women are much more likely to feel a bonding feeling that will be interpreted as love. The study found that men will usually take much longer to reach that stage of a bonding feeling. Now the name most people attach to these 3 steps is the world famous word we call LOVE or falling in LOVE. They or should I say Western culture has defined a chemical addiction as love but now this person who you have agreed to move in with or perhaps even marry is based on this sometimes false interpretation called love. Now let me be clear I am in no way saying that this is the basis for all interactions between couples, I am aware that along this time period there comes into play like admiration, appreciation as well as sacrifices to accommodate each other comfort zones, in other words there is a lot more involved besides just hormones. Having said that when one reaches this third stage there should be some honest questions of the person in the mirror. Is this person the best possible person for you? Will they have the capacity to be a good parent, a good provider, counselor and most of all a good and caring spouse intelligent enough to improve or maintain your status in life or cast you into a world of poverty, misery or even abuse? Wow! That's a pretty risky roll of the dice to be based of emotional feelings, no wonder Western love marriages have such a high divorce rate. Let's just compare these behaviors to other addictions, alcohol, cocaine and heroin. Alcohol addiction is influenced by the secretion of endorphins such as Dopamine in the brain which brings about a feeling of pleasure or euphoria and reduction of pain, it's easy to see why people can become trapped to something that makes them feel so good yet makes them prone to make terrible decisions like driving a car or aggressive behaviors that leads to fights or misspoken words. Cocaine and Heroin addictions main culprit is Dopamine; its consumption sends high levels of this hormone Dopamine into your brain causing a high sense of pleasure some addicts would choose cocaine over sex. This is one of the same hormones that are secreted during kissing and or sex. I don't need to go into each and every drug and its responses but I think you get the point. The question is are you being influenced by a powerful chemical reaction or the common sense and reasoning power of your brain which you say is "Intelligent" isn't this why you chose him or her but are you really using this thing called intelligence? Let's examine in the next chapter why the Creator/Designer put these chemicals in our bodies and for what purpose.

Survival of Our Species

Scientist today estimate that there are at least 6.5 million different species that live on land and about 2.5 in our oceans, as well as thousands being discovered each year. One thing that most of these species have in common is reproduction capabilities in the form of sex. The female will usually be the main caretakers while the males share in protection and territory rights. In the previous chapters we covered how in human relationships there are several stages before this bonding or attachment faze begins and how certain chemicals are released that some scientist call love chemicals such as dopamine and the powerful oxytocin chemicals are released to form almost an addictive bonding behavior between the two. For what reason and what is the big picture here? The survival of the human species is at stake. Take for example the Great White Shark one of the most feared creatures on the planet that's been roving about our oceans for thousands of years; however when the mother gives birth to anywhere between 2 to 12 little sharks the mother goes on her merry way without the slightest concern for their survival. The little sharks are totally independent and immediately start hunting for food minutes after birth and instinctively get as far away from the mother as possible before they end up in her belly for breakfast. On the other hand there is a large land mammal that inhabits many of the world's forests called the Black Bear, it is very protective and attentive to its young cubs until about 17 months after birth when they are finally mature enough to hunt and defend themselves. Now we know humans and most mammals and birds take meticulous care for their young, so what is it that they have that those Great White Sharks don't The answer is a good supply of dopamine and oxytocin among others chemicals released from their brains. Now what do you think would happen if humans or most animals didn't have these bonding agents released, well common sense will tell you we and or the animals wouldn't be around to tell our stories because we don't come out of the womb ready to hunt or defend ourselves like baby Great White sharks. Our very existence depends on these bonding chemicals and our reactions to them. Most of us call this reaction Romantic Love. This next statement I will repeat from time to time and that is, "The only true and real love is Unconditional Love" that is very difficult to develop between two strangers. But the question now is why we humans feel the need to build cultures and institutions around the family circle which seems to be the raising of our children resulting in schools, playgrounds, sports, hospitals, toys and youth programs. Again let's go back to the animal kingdom for some insight. I mentioned before the Great White sharks are born ready to survive and hunt the minute they are born, the Black bear cubs are cared for until they are trained to hunt and survive at 17 months, the African lion is ready to hunt and care for itself at 2 and half to 3 years and is protected by a family unit called the pride. The Golden Eagles little eaglets are full grown and ready to hunt in just over 4 months, their parents often fly back into their area just to check up on them. The closest mammals to humans, the Bush gorillas in Africa stay with their mothers and fathers for 10 to 13 years before they are ready to start a family of their own. The human baby in our Western society is not fully emancipated until 16 to 18 years before at the very least they can find employment and housing on their own, and if they are fortunate they go to college and may not leave home until after college at the age of 22. So clearly this human baby needs a whole system and lots of time to help nourish and develop it into a viable and productive addition to the adult population. From early times when most humans were in the so called hunter/gatherer stages of our human timeline the children had to learn to hunt and defend at a much earlier age but still for the first ten to twelve years they were highly dependent on the mother and father for everything. So could that be the reason why the Creator/Designer programmed those powerful chemicals into our DNA. We humans take a long time to develop so therefore we must understand the only real reason for sex is procreation or duplication of the species. But we have turned it into a form of recreation; yes I said it "Recreation". Most of us are unaware of why we have these powerful chemicals racing through our bodies when we play this game of Romance, not knowing we are playing with a powerful and misunderstood energy. Over 70% of the average teenager in the US has had sex by the age of 19 and 15% have tried it before the age of 15. But can you blame them if they are born into a society filled with sexual impulses from ads and just about any form of media available to them from infancy. I am in no way against sex or family life, my concern is the **Selection** process in this culture that has produced the following scenario. By the age of 22 years almost 50% of children will witness the divorce of their mother and father. Nearly 50% of all marriage's end within 10 years but why is this this number so high, again the selection process is way out of balance and focus. I covered the word origin and definition of the word "Romance" earlier and it plays a significant part in the selection process especially in Occidental/Western cultures, let's go into further detail in the next chapter.

The Culture of Selection

Let's now decode a few selection methods that have developed over the past 100 years or so of western culture. At the turn of the century in many small towns and rural areas in America where most people lived, the so called old school method was established that the parents where heavily involved in the selection process whereby they would suggest or approve a certain young man in the village or town who was strong and worked hard alongside his father and showed promise of the same type of discipline. He was a Christian and always said "yes Sir" or "yes Maim" to his elders certainly he would be a good candidate for someone's daughter. On the other hand the daughter's ringing qualifications were, pleasing to the eye, could read, virgin and a upstanding church going Christian that knew her way around the kitchen and obedient to her father and had promising child bearing hips. Forgive them but they were not into political correctness back then. They would eventually be introduced and go on several chaperoned dates before they could be trusted to be anywhere alone. The first kiss had to be a clandestine adventure because each family had to protect its reputation and family name. Teenage premarital sex or pregnancy would tarnish you forever in those small towns. Often times as the young couple sat on the front porch you can bet somebody was keeping a watchful eye on them. Those white wedding dresses meant something back then. Finally he decides this is the best of the lot of available women of his group and decides to approach the father for permission to marry his daughter. Father says yes, mother agrees with father and now the wedding is planned. What was the divorce rate back in the early 1900's? According to the Center for Disease Control it was hovering around 0.8%. Wow! That's awfully low I wonder why, we'll get back to that later. However these divorce numbers began to rise; from 1901 to 1942 it had skyrocketed to 24%. One reason many social scientists point to its rise was the advent of increasingly popular new technology made available to the masses. The advent of media such as radio and the motion picture industry better known as Hollywood was in its infancy stages. Because these two mediums were so readily available to mass audiences across the country the population was exposed to stories and programs that would serve as an outlet for one to partake in escapism into the fantasy world of fame and celebrity. This in time would lead to new options as far as entertainment. So now this new energetic field led people to believe it was normal to be entertained. Now they can see life in a new fictionalized format. But what did this do for the culture of the small rural towns and villages I mentioned in the beginning of this chapter. Since it was the big cities like Boston, Chicago, New York and Los Angeles that were at the forefront of these new entertainment industries its curious popularity began to spread to the rural and country areas of America so much so that the entertainment industry were accused of ruining traditional culture and values. Did they have a point? What was in these entertainment mediums that caused a change in not only American culture but European western culture as well? By 1916 there were 21,000 movie theaters in the US. The major movie and radio programs were comprised of dramas, adventures, love stories and mysteries. Most of the dramas, love stories and adventures had one central theme, a leading male actor and a leading female actress. The advertisement for these programs were plastered all over billboards and sign posts throughout city streets and storefront showcases, magazines and newspapers always showing dynamic illustrations of beautiful women and handsome leading male actors. The movie or radio shows would depict these leading characters in the story line as daring adventurous and often the male was a hero who surmounted almost impossible odds to rescue his lovely damsel in distress and they would run off and get married and live happily ever after in the end. This same scenario was played over and over only the names changed, Charlie Chaplin, Clark Gable, Humphrey Bogart, Greta Garbo, Cary Grant, Rita Hayworth, Sean Connery and Marilyn Monroe. In today's audiences it's Robert Pattinson, Bradley Cooper, Jennifer Lawrence, Denzel Washington and Kerry Washington, Halle Berry. They were all the stereotypical handsome and beautiful faces that young impressionable audiences looked up to as their mental blueprint of what they would add to their selection portfolio along with their expectations of dashing and heroic personalities. The middle class and poor became addicted to this genre of films. The young men no longer seriously considered a bride based off her talents or attributes, but physical looks and personality were placed at the top. The women not only wanted a man of financial means but he had to be dashing and handsome, a great father and husband was pushed further down the list, just because he could father children it was foolishly assumed he would be a great father. From 1901 to 1976 the divorce rate has gone from 0.8%, can you even grasp that not even 1%, to a staggering 50% with the added introduction of network television in the 1950s. The culture and selection process took a turn for the worst case. Romanticism had become the focal point in Hollywood. Earlier I covered the Romanticism movement of the 1800s the artistic, literary and intellectual movement that emphasized **feelings** over **rational thought**. This is the main formula for network TV and Hollywood, their ability to make you feel something, even though in the end we knew it wasn't real. American culture became addicted to "Feeling". I remember I took my daughters to see the movie Titanic and a dramatic scene towards the end showed Leonardo DiCaprio slowly sinking into the dark artic waters as he released Kate Winslet's hands due to severe hypothermia, I glanced over at my two daughters and saw the tears flowing down their cheeks, they felt the moment of loss and hopelessness. They along with me wanted romantic love to be the determining factor in Rose's (Kate Winslet) decision to be with poor penniless Jack Dawson (Leonardo DiCaprio) over her rich husband to be Cal Hockley (Billy Zane). If Jack would have survived he had nothing to offer her but romantic love and a few clever sketches, she would have had to support him for she had the wealth. Emotional feeling over rational thought is the poison pill taken during the selection process. A true master must not allow the body a.k.a. (dopamine, norepinephrine and oxytocin) to control the mind (rational mind). Just take a look around us now and see the results. For example look at all of the highly successful business men/women, professional male/female athletes, Rap stars and Hollywood actors; do you see physically unattractive overweight women or men by their sides? Of course not because that would not fit the "story line" or "blueprint" but it is to be noted that those professions have an even higher divorce rate than the rest of society. The so called unattractive, overweight women or men who would have been excellent choices for a spouse or partner were overlooked because they didn't fit the "storyline" or "blueprint". The biggest mistake men and women make in the selection process is the physical blueprint that has been fed to them since childhood from television and Hollywood. The women in our society are not as deeply committed to physical attributes as the men are. I know personally men who were dissatisfied with their wives weight gain after marriage especially after a women's first child to the point where they constantly body shamed their wives because they are not following the blue print, which in turn gives him an excuse to become unfaithful with the "blueprint girl" this often leads to marital problems and divorce. However the women more than often will accept weight gain in their men as long as he is bringing home the bacon and be attentive to family needs. In fact she feels more confident because the less attractive he is to other women the better for her and the family. So as we look at the landscape of this problem we see that it is deeply systemic. As Morpheus would say in the movie The Matrix "we are born into the matrix" we can't be blamed for the system we are born into. A mother duck naturally sees to it that her little ducklings are born near water and walks them to the water for their first swimming lesson. However humans are born into an environment that constantly changes according to the whims of those who control the environment. Can this situation be altered? Yes anything can change but first you have to have something to offer in exchange for what you have now. The selection process in the western culture has led to various options which are approached much like the medical industry approaches its practice. Our society places its energy on treating the symptoms rather than the root cause. This situation may have a remedy in a most dramatic and radical fashion. In the Occidental societies which include the Americas North South America as well as Europe let's see if there are any differences in the success rate of marriages. Our neighbors to the north Canada according to Divorce Magazine dated 2015 is about 41%, United States 45%, Sweden 54%, United Kingdom 42%, Germany 39%. So on the average 4 out of 10 marriages will end within 10 years. But Western society is not the only society on this planet is there? Let's take a peek into some different cultures that have been in place for thousands of years. In the Eastern culture the divorce rate in China has been increasing the last 7 years its national average is now 2.2%, that's awfully low. India's divorce rate has been rising lately also it's now up to 1.3%. China and India comprise over a third of the world's population of 7.6 billion and despite several attempts from foreign invaders to change their culture they have maintained their religions and culture. What is it they have that Western societies don't? Well you may not want to hear this but the answer is simply **Arranged Marriage.** WHAT!! 99.9% of Americans would absolutely reject this notion within 2 seconds flat. I'm not saying this is a quick fix for American culture because it has taken use over 100 years to go from 0.8% divorce rate to 45%. But remember in India and China divorce was virtually unheard of 100 years ago. What makes arranged marriages vs romantic love marriages much more successful? Well as I covered in the beginning of this chapter how the American family was involved in the selection process and they influenced the choices to someone who they felt was a suitable match for their son/daughter. Today the family is just about the last to know you're even in love with someone until you decide to bring them to Thanksgiving dinner or the family barbeque to meet them, by then it's too late because no matter what they say against the union you have your mind made up that this is your soul mate, your one and only true love. In many parts of India and Asia where the predominant religions are Hinduism, Buddhism and Islam the following is considered normal protocol; most couples who their families have matched together do not date, they may spend 30 minutes meeting each other and then wed within 6 months or after they finish college. In many of these cultures it is the parent's scared duty to marry their children to good families. In some parts of India the couples are allowed to go on a few dates to get to know each other a little better. Now most people in America have mostly negative feelings about arranged marriages, oops! There goes that word again "feeling" but numbers don't lie. Many in the West think that most of these marriages are forced, however the only country that allows forced marriages is Afghanistan and parts of Pakistan. Do the couples have to accept the arranged partners? No in most countries that sanction these arrangements the consent of the parties involved is necessary. One fact most people are not aware of that even in the British Royal Family the consented marriage of Prince Harry and Megan Markel was governed by "The Succession of the Crown Act" signed into law 2013. This states that the 6 descendants in line from the Queen had to have permission from the Sovereign Queen Elizabeth or else Prince Harry would have to choose another partner if she (The Queen) would have rejected her. Prince Harry and Megan are 6th in line for the crown. The next question most Americans will ask is, what about love? Since arranged marriages are not based on romantic love doesn't mean that in time true love can grow and most often it does. Now I am in no way suggesting that as of today overnight in order to lower the divorce rate Western societies should resort to arranged marriages. This is something that is deeply integrated in a culture for thousands of years, as well as the notion that divorce is the absolute last solution in these cultures as they will most likely stay in the marriage long enough to work things out. So what is the long term solution? Well are we going to sit around and wait another 100 years to find out? I think we are smart enough to figure out that this present selection process is pushing a 45% failure rate. I just went over the statistics on the divorce rates of cultures with extremely low percentages. Now remember in 1901 Western Culture had percentages of less than 1%, amazing right. So let's analyze a few points here. Remember it was the input from the family in the selection process and the approval of the family that was paramount in the decision, the young man had to go to the family of the girl for approval as well as the young man's family had to approve of women as well and believe me the families knew well the reputations of the small town families and if the families were against the union it most likely won't happen due to information gathered about the suiter. That's why you heard stories of couples who would "Elope" or run away secretly and get married because the parents did not approve. In small towns and villages the church was and still is the number one face to face evaluation and gossip center. The families in the eastern countries like India, China, Malaysia and Japan take pride in their most important duty to make sure their daughters and sons were wed to families that were not only beneficial to the bride and groom but also to the two families involved. So there had to be some data gathered that would insure this union was beneficial. The one thing that was not allowed to cloud this judgement was "Feelings" or the chemical secretions that encourage lust, sex, attachment, all which have very little to do with choosing the correct spouse for building a solid foundation for a successful marriage. In western culture the family is told to mind their own business when it comes to the lives of their newly wedded children especially since they had no part in the selection process. The bride and groom having any problems are told they should go to some total strangers called Marriage Counselors to solve their issues. By the way it falls up under the Family Therapist industry which generates billions of dollars in revenue yearly. So how has Western Society managed this problem of near 50% rate of divorce? They don't, they take full advantage of it by commercializing it. Let's take a look at the Divorce Industry.

Rinse and Repeat

There was a time in America when the shoe repair industry was booming. The shoe makers before the 80s use to make men's and women's shoes out of high grade leather uppers as well as leather soles, if your heel or sole of your shoe began to wear out it was normal to take them to the local shoe shop and have the worn heel or sole replaced. The thought of replacing the whole shoe sometimes didn't happen unless the upper part of the shoe was just plain worn out, torn and dull. My father and some of my uncles had shoes they had worn for 15 to 20 years. Well in today's world if you get a scratch or mark on your 3 month old sneakers they are tossed or sold on EBay and a new model is purchased with just a short trip to the local mall. Most women rarely wear the same pair of pumps twice. Well today's solution to marriage in the western society is damn near about the same, after a short time dealing with a spouse's drama or indifference a divorce lawyer is summoned to offer his or her solution, and ladies and gents it aint free, have you noticed what types of cars divorce attorney's drive. The Divorce Industry has averaged over 50 billion dollars a year in revenue from divorce attorney's fees, filing fees, court fees and arbitrators, if your spouse decides to fight you for that vacation home in Florida your attorney fees could escalate rapidly and after the divorce is final, somebody has to move out or houses have to be sold. Real Estate agents are making money as well which translates into moving companies, storage companies to store whatever the judge awarded you until you find a new apartment or house. Lately our western culture has added some new departments to the money grabbing divorce industry; Divorce parties, yes people are now throwing themselves divorce celebrations and spending between $5,000 and $30,000, as you know liquor and drugs are taking their fair share from this off shoot market. Recording star Robin Thicke celebrated his divorce from movie actress Paula Patton in 2014 by throwing himself a lavish Divorce party complete with sexy models and celebrity friends; I'm guessing he and Paula Patton didn't share mutual friends. There is a hotel in upstate New York called "The Divorce Hotel" where couples can pay fees from $5,000 to $20,000 to check in Friday afternoon and be pampered with spa treatments, fancy restaurants indoor pools and lawyers who will have your divorce complete by the time you check out Sunday morning, it is said to take the stress out of divorce. Wow! So we have a $72 billion dollar marriage industry on one side and a $50 billion dollar industry waiting for you on the other side. One thing you can bet for sure the divorce industry is not rooting for your success in marriage. Let's not forget the precious children who are always caught in the middle of this mess and could be affected psychologically for years. Just think of what would happen if the divorce rate would fall back to 0.8%, a lot of lost revenue and jobs as well as an economic disaster. The method and aftermath of divorce is much like how the medical industry handles disease, they give treatments instead of curing the root cause, and oh how we like to give treatments. First we get the advice from our closest friends who after seeing you suffer for a while with the antics and infidelity or abuse of your spouse, their first words of advice is "leave him/her you can do better without them" or "you should seek professional counseling" and finally "I know a good divorce attorney you should see". Well it looks like 45% of the troubled couples make that fateful call to the divorce attorney, in America there are on average one divorce every 36 seconds, over 16,000 per week and nearly 900,000 per year. The sad part about it is more than half of these divorcees will repeat this process again without understanding the real dynamics behind the process of their failure. I take my hat off to those couples in the 55% percent who worked through the process and decided to stick it out despite the odds and society working against them. Now another note to this whole situation is nobody keeps stats on those couples who never get married and breakup so those numbers could vary greatly. However one thing is certain, they probably used the Romantic Love formula which has proven to have a low success rate. I will say it again the only true love is "Unconditional love" Now I know there are some successful marriages that started off in the romantic love concept but they were able to swim against the strong current of opposition and through self-discovery they made it to the shores of Unconditional Love, but not many make it do they. Let's now focus on the concepts of love. Unconditional love verses conditional love. Romantic love is 99% based on certain conditions that have to be met on a consistent basis for example you may hear these concerns as time goes by; "You don't open the door for me anymore" or "You used to hold my hand and kiss in public" or "You used to tell me you love me all the time" "We haven't had sex in over 6 months". The list goes on and on because in the beginning the couple is playing the "Romantic Game" in order to lure the other into its agenda which is vague in the beginning of a relationship because they are both going off how they make each other feel instead of asking the real questions, but that is what makes the whole thing slippery even if you ask the real questions many won't be honest in the beginning, if he or she is visibly financially well off and you ask the question "Are with me for my money?" I doubt you will get an honest answer especially if he or she was waiting tables at your favorite restaurant when you met. But eventually their actions will reveal the truth. When you have a relationship based on conditional romantic love when certain conditions are not met the boat starts to get rocky does it not. The biggest complaint I here from people after they begin to have problems is the following. "If I had known you were like this I would have never married you" Remember the definition of Romance *"A fabulous relation or story of adventures and incidents designed for the entertainment of readers; a tale of extraordinary adventures, fictitious and often extravagant, usually a tale of love or war.. It vaults and soars beyond the limits of fact and real life."* Hollywood and television has sewn into the fabric of our society this program that for the most part is unrealistic. You don't need to be in love to get married, love especially romantic love should be later in the relationship after it has been established and has a foundation. Example let's say you know someone who has the same aspirations to become successful in their career choice and you both love children and outdoor gardening, you come to an agreement that you could help each other get your College degrees buy a house get married birth and raise some children and have a beautiful outdoor garden and along the way they fall in love. Your original goal does not depend on "Feelings" and at the end of the first phase of the goal of getting your degrees if you decided not to go forward at the very least you have helped each other progress. Partnership with a distinct goal in mind not based off love but because you really want and enjoy working and being together as you work towards your goal. Now when you have those children then you will now understand what "Unconditional Love" is. I have seen countless examples of the trials and sacrifices of parents extending themselves never questioning their devotion to their children no matter how they behave towards them. Unconditional love takes years of sweat to develop for your spouse however for ones newborn child it can be a matter of seconds. In order to have a successful long lasting relationship or marriage the selection process has to be refined and cannot be based off superficial fantasies we have accepted as normal, they just don't have a high success rate, the numbers don't lie. So what are the other options? Well our society has come up with a few in the last 30 years.

Changes on the Horizon ?

In the early 1900's with the advent of new technologies such as the radio and on to early days of motion pictures and into the heavily commercialized industry of television networks we have witnessed swift evolution in the way women and men interact with each other affecting traditions and cultures worldwide. In a short span of rapid advances in electronic technology we went from the early introduction to television sets to the mass population around 1950 where in the United States less than one million people had a television set in their homes. That number would rise to 44 million by 1969, and as of today nearly 98% of American households have at least one television set. Electronic technologies have become a worldwide multi-trillion dollar industry. According to statistica.com in the 1984 the average amount of households in America with PC's or personal computers was 8% today it has mushroomed into nearly 95% with various forms such as laptops, tablets and of course the smartphone which has an enormous amount of computing power compared to it early flip phone versions. How has this new wave of technology affected the marriage selection process? This new form of media introduced the world to a new form of technology unlike one way forms of media such as radio, motion pictures, television and music recordings, this new technology has birthed a new concept. Interactive forms of media that could actually respond to you. Online Dating, yes a service much like online shopping except these pair of shoes can actually talk back show you pictures and even set up a meet and greet at your local Starbucks. In the comfort of your living room in your pajamas you can stroll through and sample thousands of member profiles that includes pictures, pets, and interesting things they say about themselves (all positive of course) who live in all parts of the world. Worldwide there are over 8,000 such sites and over 3,500 in the United States with the most popular ones being sites such as Match.com, eHarmony.com, Plentyoffish.com, Tinder, Grinder and OkCupid are among the largest ones according to Online Dating Magazine. In the beginning people were skeptical and often called such relationships superficial or even desperate people who were uncomfortable with interacting with people face to face. So could this be the answer to the dilemma of high divorce rates, let see what the so called experts say. Michael Rosenfeld is a sociologist at Stanford University who has conducted a long running study of 3,000 people and his findings are promising. He says the online experience gives them more potential partners then they would have if it was just left up to chance meetings or meeting through friends or family suggestions. In his study he reveals that people who meet online are less likely to break up within the first year. He discovered that people who meet online tend to marry faster because they are able to look for characteristics that they know they're going to like, in short you are able to gather a lot more information about that person then you would with an offline relationship, even before the first live meet and greet you have already moved past some initial hurdles. He also found that members of such sites like Match.com and eHarmony are more intent on finding long term quality partners with similar backgrounds. According to Statistics Brain Research Institute 1 in 6 marriages start online. Another development to online dating was exposed by The Pew Research Center's revelation that over 80% of participants are open to interracial relationships that could lead to marriage. This form of media allows people of different racial backgrounds to intermingle in private and non-judgmental settings that they would perhaps never have had such exposure to. Well let's get down to the proverbial "Meat and Potatoes" how has this affected to divorce rate? Let's go to our professional researchers who make living answering questions like the following. What are your chances of a more successful marriage if you meet online instead of offline? I found various answers to that question; let's start with Professor John Cacioppo from the University of Chicago. His research involved a Harris Poll of nearly 20,000 Americans who got married between 2005 and 2012. It found that 35% of them met online. 8% of those who did not meet online were divorced while just 6% of the couples who met and married online were divorced. He also noted that the higher the income the more likely they met their partners online. The study also found an increase in marital satisfaction among people who meet online. A counter opinion to that study was given by Dr. Eli Finkel a professor of social psychology at Northwestern University comments that while "The study is a good one" "But any conclusions that online marriages are better is premature" Dr. Finkel believes there should be more study in this field before conclusions can be drawn. Now the National Academy of Sciences magazine called Proceedings a non-profit organization made up of the countries leadings researchers found that as of 2013 the 19,131 couples who met online only 7% were divorced compared to the nearly 50% national divorce rate. Again this is a new field of research and it may take many more years of data to draw any definite conclusions.

This next compilation of data may be biased and probably is but there are sites such as Match.com and eHarmony that include extensive questioners and psychological examinations particular eHarmony.com. Their sites and are more focused on members who are not looking for the casual hookup like Tinder or Grinder. This is the data that eHarmony touts as there results from members of their online dating site. While Match.com is geared toward long term relationships as well as casual and is open to the LGBT community, eHarmony is strictly about long term and marriage and excludes the LGBT community entirely; they also do not allow you to browse through other members profiles. There entire selection process is put into the electronical hands of its computer programs algorithm once you complete its compatibility test. They will then give you a list of your compatible choices but you can't interact until you have paid for your membership. What type of results do they boast from this process? According to the website DatingAdvice.com reports eHarmony's success rate is as follows; over 70% of men and women who join the site find their spouse on eHarmony, 15 million matches a day are created on its site, eHarmony is responsible for near 4% of US marriages, they also claim that over 600,000 of its members have gotten married. The divorce rate of couples who met on eHarmony is just 3.86% as of September 2016. Wow! That's amazing if you can believe eHarmony stats. If those stats hold up over the next 10 to 20 years that would be a big improvement over the nearly 50% divorce rate now. With all of these marriages these online websites and apps are generating are we in danger of creating a boom in marriages that could ultimately lead to a near epidemic in divorces in the near future, why do I say this, well remember in the chapter "Culture of Selection" the selection process slowly changed from common sense to emotional feelings with the advent of technology via radio, motion pictures and television. The one thing that never changed was the base ingredient of "ROMANTIC LOVE" if you use that as your primary ingredient would be tantamount to thinking cotton candy on a hot summer day at the fair will not melt in your hands before you got home. Only those who rely on unconditional love or rational selection can make it through that, and that's roughly 50%. Whether its eHarmony, Grinder or Match.com the handsome guy in the frozen foods section or the pretty lady you met at church if it starts out on our cultures fascination with romantic love it's a near 50-50 proposition. Now maybe online dating gives you more of a chance of finding someone who is more compatible based on a collection of more data and could aid in possibly making a more rational decision instead of an emotional one made when the mind and body is flooded with automatic hormones that you misdiagnose as some magical potion defined as love. If you are reading this book right now and wondering what happened to your last relationship or marriage and wonder why it didn't last, stop the blame game, you were both duped into the fantasy of a wonderful story line that neither one of you could continue to play it's leading characters any longer or in 90% of the time one person just couldn't play the role any longer. You remember those arguments and lamentations of "Why can't we go back to how it was in the beginning?" It will never be what it was in the beginning because you were living the fictitious story lines written by Hollywood and played over and over again since you were infants. This society needs to learn something from other parts of human society and recognize that we can take bits and pieces from societies who do have a high success rates in marriage. Western culture does not have all the answers or a Utopian society. Now I know what you're thinking. That I'm suggesting arranged marriages is the only solution. What I am saying in order to improve our way of life for the sake of our society and to increase the cohesiveness of the family unit the divorce rate has got to come way down! Remember it was 0.8% in 1901 just think of how much stronger today's family unit would be if it had stayed that low. Our children have to be educated on a productive understanding and philosophy on how to choose a mate who not only is beneficial to each other but to each other's families and eventually our society as a whole. The cookie cutter examples we have shown them the past 100 years is resulted in broken families frustrated and damaged children who continue the same cycle. In turn it has spawned a $50 billion a year divorce industry, just think of all the children we could send to higher education and disease prevention with 50 billion dollars each year we don't have to feed to the divorce attorneys who speed by us in their high priced luxury cars and yachts.

Conclusion

Chances are that 50% of the readers of this book have either been divorced or are children of parents who are divorced. This is the silent virus that nobody talks about because it has become such an acceptable part of our society, almost like mass shootings nobody thinks it will happen to them yet people still justify we should all have guns and oddly enough nobody seems to find a gun when these mass shooting occur. I digress I was only a few miles away from the Parkland High School shootings in Florida when it happened in 2018. But have we become a society where abnormal or destructive patterns become acceptable behavior. When are we going to take action? We certainly can't lay the entire burden on politicians and law makers; they can only do so much. The clock is ticking as we speak every 13 seconds there is a divorce in America. But despite the bad press divorce has given to marriage lets give a standing ovation to those couples who did not depend on fairy tale romance to sustain them over the years they stayed with it because they saw in it something bigger that just a feeling or something to brag about, they stayed with it because that was their mission in life to raise a family together and along the way learned about life and the ultimate goal of unconditional love, the only true love there is. Now when I say unconditional love I don't mean to the point of unhealthy physical or mental abuse of you by your partner, self-preservation is always the first and oldest law of nature. If you find yourself in this situation there are all kinds of organizations that are available to you, but first you must break to mental chains that keep you captive. You must come to a realization that the present system you have grown up in from infancy has taught you that since your marriage was performed by a Pastor or Bishop that somehow God have put some magical holy bond of some unbreakable spell on your marriage. I say somebody lied on God because God has given man free will to experience life on his/her terms and decisions, if you say your marriage was blessed by God then why will 16,000 divorces happen this week alone, so please don't blame the preacher because he didn't perform the ceremony correctly, remember it was you who made the choice to marry this person and what reasons you put into the decision was all yours based on your environment and frame of mind, one of which you had no say in. So I ask you to reexamine how you will come to the decision to marry your first or next husband/wife. Will it be based off the societal cultural norm that everyone from your favorite entertainer, athlete, actor, or family member has chosen or are you going to break this chain and choose "Wisely" what is best for not only you but your family and your spouse's family as well. Will you break the mold and make your selection in the vacuum of a sound mind and not based off the sexual primal injections meant to bind you for rearing children together, remember you are not "Hunter Gatherers" anymore you are in a controlled environment with standing armies and police forces well fed and paid to keep you safe so that you can make well rounded and rational choices without fear of being invaded by enemy tribes. So you must reason if you want to go to art school and open an art gallery you will be severely side tracked if you allow yourself to fall into a Romantic Love relationship with a career criminal who will keep you trapped in the web of Chemical Love, for this criminal can do nothing but burden you and your family to the point of financial ruin. Sadly similar scenarios play out like this over and over again. The recipe is as good as its ingredients, however it's time for you to stop copying someone else's recipe and make up your own for success. There is no excuse to continue with the same recipe with ingredients that will make 45% of you literally sick to your stomach. Over 100 years of history has revealed to us where and why this took a drastic turn from a 99% success rate to an unacceptable 55% success rate. There is far too much information at our disposal for this to continue. However sadly there are two industries that make a combined total of $122 billion dollars off of our ignorance of why we haphazardly sleep walk through the same scenario over and over thinking our plight will somehow have a different outcome. A famous author and lecturer Terence McKenna once said, "The main thing to understand is that we are imprisoned in some kind of work of art" my interpretation of that is, if one doesn't somehow take the paint brush out of someone else's hands we will continue to be painted into a corner by the designs of something other than our wishes. Wake up! Remove this heavy veil of darkness we call tradition and culture. So much of our culture has changed, some say for the better some say for the worst, it depends what side of the fence your standing on I suppose. I think you'll agree with me that when it comes to our family, health of our society and its only resource for its future our children it's time to consider some real changes. I don't profess to know a definitive answer for all people that would be a foolish attempt considering the cascade of religious, political and various ethnicities involved. The track record of marriages based solely on Romantic love has proven to have a weak foundation and short shelf life. Our society and culture does not and probably would never accept Arranged marriages, one reason being is that we believe that freedom means choice, I have talked to many married men and women who feel trapped instead of free. Maybe online selection with the aid of computer algorithms will sweep us all into a world based off a highly sophisticated data driven selection system that the latest generation will somehow use as a guideline for success, let's hope they are at least on track for a better system than what we have now.

"The syntactical nature of reality, the real secret of magic, is that the world is made of words. And if you know the words that the world is made of, you can make of it whatever you wish."

Terence McKenna

Bibliography

- Oxford Dictionary of English © Oxford University Press, 2010, 2017.
- Western Culture, **https://en.wikipedia.org/wiki/West ern_culture**. Accessed 4/22/2019
- Romance; The American Dictionary of the English Language by Noah Webster 1828. **ISBN:** 091249803X, **ISBN-13:** 9780912498034
- Brides.com online magazine August 31st 2017, by Meredith Lepore. https://www.brides.com/story/this-is-how-long-most-couples-date-before-getting-married. Accessed 4/22/2019
- Examined Existence online magazine, Why We Fall in Love: The Science of Love, Brain Health and Functionality. https://examinedexistence.com/why-we-fall-in-love-the-science-of-love. Accessed 5/4/2019
- Encyclopedia Britannica 250th Anniversary, online edition,

https://www.britannica.com/art/his
tory-of-the-motion-picture/The-
silent-years-1910-27. Accessed
5/4/2019

- Divorce Magazine.com updated June
  20th 2019.
  https://www.divorcemag.com/article
  s/world-divorce-statistics-page-1/
  accessed 6/22/2019

- Wikipedia.org Succession to the
  Crown Act 2013.
  https://en.wikipedia.org/wiki/Succ
  ession to the Crown Act 2013.
  Citation c. 20. Introduced by Nick
  Clegg

- Vanity Fair.com
  https://www.vanityfair.com/hollywo
  od/2014/10/robin-thicke-divorce-
  party. October 15th 2014. Accessed
  5/22/2019

- The Divorce Hotel.
  https://www.divorcehotel.com/

- Statista.com
  https://www.statista.com/statistic
  s/214641/household-adoption-rate-
  of-computer-in-the-us-since-1997/.
  Accessed 5/25/2019

- http://healthland.time.com/2013/06/03/more-satisfaction-less-divorce-for-people-who-meet-spouses-online/. Accessed 5/25/2019

- https://web.stanford.edu/~mrosenfe/Rosenfeld How Couples Meet Working Paper.pdf. Published in the American Sociological Review 77(4): 523-547 2012

- Dating Advice.com, writer Hayley Matthews dated 9/30/2016 https://www.datingadvice.com/online-dating/eharmony-success-rate

- PNAS (Proceedings of the National Academy of Sciences) https://doi.org/10.1073/pnas.1222447110. John T. Cacioppo, Stephanie Cacioppo, Gian C. Gonzaga, Elizebeth L. Ogburn and Tyler J. VanderWeele. June 18, 2013

- US Department of Health Education and Welfare, 100 years of marriage and Divorce statistics United States. DHEW Publication (HRA)74-1902

Uaxsaktun Publishers Private
uaxsaktunpublishers@gmail.com

www.ingramcontent.com/pod-product-compliance
Lightning Source LLC
Chambersburg PA
CBHW020608030426
42337CB00013B/1275